Eocene

Jurassic
193,000,000 years ago

Triassic
225,000,000 years ago   Conifers and ferns

Permian
280,000,000 years ago   Deciduous plants appear

Carboniferous
345,000,000 years ago   Thick forests of giant
                                         evergreens (these are coal-
                                         forming forests)

Devonian
395,000,000 years ago   Plants with roots, stems
                                         and leaves appear on land.
                                         First forests

Silurian
435,000,000 years ago   Leafless plants on land

Ordovician
500,000,000 years ago   Plant life in sea

Cambrian
570,000,000 years ago   Plant life in sea

Pre-Cambrian   Beginning of life in sea.
                                         Algae and seaweeds common

Miocene

Pleistocene

This book will introduce you to the science of Botany
— the study of plants.

There are about half a million different kinds of plants on our planet, and each one is a living thing with its own special way of growing and surviving. A simple hand magnifying glass will take you into a whole new world.

Acknowledgments
The authors and publishers wish to acknowledge the following additional illustrative material:
pages 9, 22 and 24 — photographs by Tim Clark; page 33 — photograph by John Moyes; pages 16, 43 and 46 — photographs by the Natural History Photographic Agency; page 41 — photograph by Oxford Scientific Films Ltd; page 10 — illustration by Ian Rawlings; pages 19, 20 and 30 — photographs by Harry Stanton; pages 5, 8, 32, 34, 44, 45, 47 and 48 — photographs by M M Whitehead.

First edition

© LADYBIRD BOOKS LTD MCMLXXXIII

An introduction to
Botany

by JOHN and DOROTHY PAULL

illustrated by BRIAN PRICE THOMAS
and DRURY LANE STUDIOS

Ladybird Books Loughborough

The Science of Botany

We live on a very beautiful planet. In some areas where the soil is rich and the climate mild, lots of different plants grow packed together. Plants do not grow everywhere, however; there are huge desert regions where thousands of square kilometres are bare of plants.

Studying plants is a pleasant and relaxing hobby. Some people think that only exotic greenhouse plants are interesting. They miss the beauty of common plants that grow in woodlands, hedgerows, meadows and even in pavement cracks. Learning about such plants can be fascinating.

Dandelion

This book is about the plant kingdom and introduces you to Botany — the study of plants. When you have read it, try to get to know the plants around you by taking regular walks. Armed with a good reference book to help to name plants, you can quickly get to know the wild flowers in your neighbourhood. Keep a notebook and write down anything interesting you see. Put the date and the place where you find each plant in the notebook. Remember: do not pick wild flowers. We need to leave the countryside as we find it so that others can enjoy the beauty of the plants.

Purple Orchid

Eocene plant fossil

Different kinds of plants

Altogether there are about half a million different kinds of plants growing on our planet.

Plants, like all forms of life, trace their origins back to the sea. The beginnings of plant life are lost in the mists of time, because fossils do not appear in any quantity until about 600,000,000 years ago. Plant remains that have been discovered do not mean that life suddenly appeared at that particular time. They tell us only that living organisms did not acquire hard parts capable of preservation until then.

No one knows exactly how or when life began in the sea, but it is thought that the first simple plants lived about 2,000,000,000 years ago.

About 420,000,000 years ago, plants were able to survive on land. The first land plants probably did not have roots, but used a tangle of branch-like growths to perch on the masses of rotting seaweed thrown up from the sea. Eventually, land plants, helped by the forces of nature, decomposed the bare rocks into soil in which roots could anchor and gather water. With the passage of time, dead plants added to the soil depth, and more complex plants developed. Somehow, the ancestor of the first tree grew. From that start came forests of the simplest kinds of plants.

Relics of these primitive tree-size plants are with us today — the mosses and ferns that inhabit damp, shaded parts of the countryside.

Botanists divide plants into two main groups: the *Flowering Plants* have roots, stems, leaves, flowers and fruits, and include all our trees. Ferns, mosses, algae and fungi are *Non-Flowering Plants*.

plant life in the Mesozoic era

7

Identifying plants

Getting to know all the plants you find is not easy. Over five thousand different kinds of plants live wild in the British Isles, and most of them are uncommon. In the average country parish, you would expect to find about four hundred different plant types growing throughout the year.

Most bookshops sell natural history picture reference books that help in identification. Naming plants presents a problem, though, because some have more than one English name. Wild arum, for instance, is also known as 'cuckoo pint', 'lords and ladies', 'vicar in the pulpit', and in one county as 'kitty come down the lane, jump up and

Wild Arum
flower and berries

These berries are poisonous
DO NOT TOUCH

kiss me'! Fortunately, it has only one scientific name which is part of the international language of science, helping botanists and naturalists in one country to know what those in another country are talking about. For instance, 'cuckoo pint' might mean nothing to a botanist in Japan, but the name *Arum maculatum* certainly would. The scientific name consists normally of two Latin words, a system of classification devised by Linnaeus (1707-1778), a Swedish scientist.

Linnaeus grouped plants and animals according to similarities in their body structures.

You can learn how to identify plants when they are not in flower by looking at their structure in the way a botanist would. To do this, you will need a good quality pocket lens — an essential tool for every field botanist.

The parts of a flowering plant

Each plant has its own distinctive shape and colour which helps to identify it. Whatever their shape and size, flowering plants have the same basic features.

A buttercup (above) is a typical flowering plant. With a trowel carefully dig one up in the garden, and spread the plant out on an old newspaper. You will see that it has two main parts: the root system which grows in the earth, and the shoot system which is above the ground.

The buttercup's roots grow underground in search of water and mineral salts. As the roots probe the soil particles, they anchor the plant firmly in the earth so that the shoot system doesn't get blown over in the wind. The roots grow into the top layer of soil, but some small plants go as deep as two metres in search of water. Some woodland trees (they are flowering plants) have roots to a depth of eighteen metres.

Roots absorb mineral salts and water from the ground, and these rise through the shoot system to all parts of the plant: the leaves, the flowers, the seeds and the fruits. The water and mineral salts are needed for the plant to grow.

The plant roots also help the soil. They hold the soil particles together to stop them from being blown or washed away. The roots break up the earth as well, so that other living things, like worms and insects, can live in it.

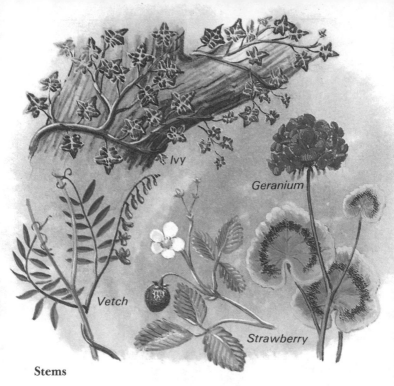

Ivy

Vetch

Geranium

Strawberry

Stems

The stem of a plant connects the roots to the leaves and flowers. Many wild plants have strong, upright stems and others have thin, weak stems. Some are tall and some are short and stubby. Thin weak-stemmed plants, like the wild strawberry, creep on the top of the soil, while strong, erect-stemmed plants, like the geranium, stand high and firm. Members of the vetch family wrap themselves around grasses and bushes. Ivy clings to tree trunks and brick walls, because it cannot support its own weight. Trees have the strongest stem: the part called the trunk.

In most plants, the stem holds the plant upright and supports the leaves in such a way that they get plenty of light from the sun. As well as holding the leaves and the flower at the top, stems carry water and salts from the earth to the flowers and leaves in little tubes. The leaves need water and mineral salts to make food when the sun is shining.

You can see how stems take dissolved salts and water from the roots by standing a stick of celery in a jar of water mixed with a teaspoonful of blue ink. Leave it for a few hours. After a while, you will see thin, blue lines in the celery stick. If you cut the stick in half carefully, you will see the blue coloured dots where the ink has passed through the narrow tubes.

Some plant stems become very swollen. This is because the plants use their stems as 'store houses'. Crocuses store food in this way.

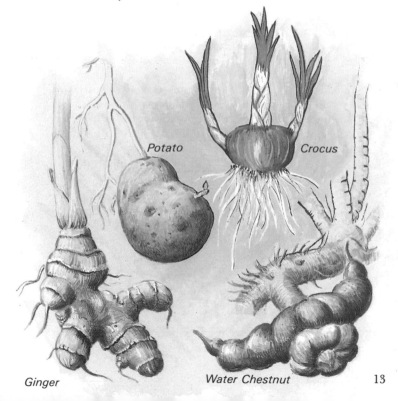

Potato

Crocus

Ginger

Water Chestnut

Roots

If you dug up a spadeful of earth in a woodland, you would find lots of thin, white roots spreading throughout the ground. The roots differ from one type of plant to another. In some plants the roots are made up of several parts growing from the lower end of the stem. These are called *fibrous roots* and they spread out in the soil and give the plants sturdy anchorage.

Take another look at the buttercup you dug from the garden. It has fibrous roots. Shake off the grains of soil in between the roots, spread the roots out on a sheet of newspaper, and look at them through a magnifying glass. Can you see tiny 'root hairs' on each root? They collect water and salts for the buttercup.

Sometimes roots are made up of one main thick root with smaller fibres growing from the sides. The thick root is called the *tap root*. Dig up a dandelion with its root intact. Instead of a cluster of roots, you will see that the dandelion plant has one tap root, unlike the buttercup. Tap roots store food for the dandelion to use the following winter. Carrots and parsnips are tap roots, and when we eat them we are eating food which the plants would have used during the cold winter months.

Stand a plant in a narrow bottle half full with water, and gently pour a thin layer of cooking oil onto the surface of the water to 'seal' it. Mark the level of the water with a felt pen. Place the bottle on a sunlit window sill and leave it for a day or two. The water level will drop because the roots absorb some of the water, which travels up the stem to the leaves and flowers. Why do we seal the surface of the water?

Most trees are deep-rooted. A mature oak has hundreds of kilometres of roots searching the soil for water and salts. Each drop of water collected by root hairs is passed along the roots to the trunk, branches and leaves.

fibrous root

tap root

15

Leaves

Look at a sycamore or oak leaf, and you will see that the leaf has a *leaf stalk* that is joined to the stem coming off the branch. The *leaf blade* is flat and smooth, and running down the centre is the main vein or *midrib*. Lots of narrow branch veins transport water and salts to the leaf. They also carry food made by the leaf to other parts of the tree.

Some leaves have smooth edges, some have wavy edges. The elm leaf has teeth-like edges. There are leaves with thin, long stalks, and leaves with short, thick stalks. Some leaves do not have stalks at all. The jagged edges help to evaporate water, to cut down wind resistance so that the leaf doesn't snap in a wind, and to act as 'drip tips' for shedding unwanted water.

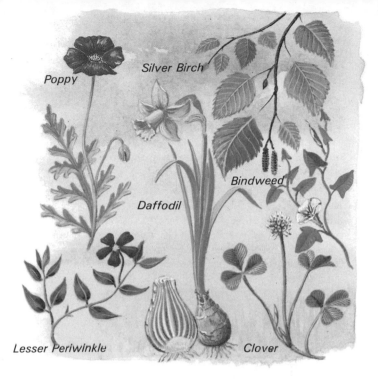

Poppy

Silver Birch

Bindweed

Daffodil

Lesser Periwinkle

Clover

Leaves manufacture food. They are sometimes called 'sugar factories'. The green colour is chlorophyll, a chemical which, with the help of light, changes carbon dioxide and water into sugars. The carbon dioxide comes from the air through small holes called *stomata*. Moisture can also be lost from these holes. When they are not in use at night, or in dry weather, they shut up to save water for the plant.

When only one leaf grows on a stalk, it is called a *simple* leaf. If a leaf blade is divided into separate parts, the leaf is a *compound* leaf.

Some plants, such as the daffodil, the tulip and the snowdrop, store the sugar they produce in special leaves packed together. These food packages are *bulbs*.

Flowers

A flower is usually the most beautiful and sweetest smelling part of a plant. It is important because it changes into seeds and fruits from which new plants grow.

Find a flower in the garden, and look at its shape and colour. Notice that the flower is attached to the stem by a stalk. In some plants the flowers grow singly, and in others they grow in bunches.

You will notice that the flower has four parts: the *petals*, the *sepals*, the *stamens* and the *carpels*. The illustration will help you to identify them. The petals are the main part of the flower. They are usually colourful. Some petals protect the flower parts from the weather, but others are large and open to attract insects. Underneath the petals is a ring of sepals which look like small leaves. These protect the flower when it is a bud, before it has opened.

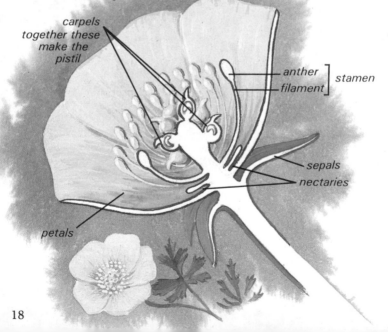

carpels together these make the pistil

anther] stamen
filament

sepals

nectaries

petals

Some flowers have lots of stamens. Each stamen has a *filament* and an *anther* on top which, when ripe, contains pollen. Each grain of pollen contains a male cell which can fertilise a female egg cell.

The female part of the flower is the *pistil*, usually found in the centre. Can you find it in your flower? The *ovary* is the swelling at the base of the flower, and inside are tiny *ovules*. Each ovule contains an egg cell. The *style* is the long, thin stalk arising from the ovary. Its tip is sticky and hairy and is called the *stigma* (see also page 21).

Many insects crawl and fly into the flower, attracted by the colour and the smell of nectar, a sugary substance made in the *nectaries*. As the tiny creatures move around the flower, they often get showered in pollen.

Dog Rose   *Rose hips*

Flowers change into fruits

Flowers do not last for ever. They change into fruits. Seeds form after pollen grains reach the egg cells inside the ovary.

This happens when ripe pollen bags burst open. The pollen grains can be carried on the backs of hairy small creatures such as bees, or they can float in the air and land on another flower.

Flowers that have their pollen collected by insects are often a special shape. This makes it easier for the insect to get into the flower to be covered with pollen. The snapdragon *(antirrhinum)*, for example, opens when a bee lands on the lower lip of the flower and the stamens shower pollen on the insect's back. A smaller insect would not get into the flower since its weight would not push down the lower lip.

Other plants, such as grasses, oaks, poplars, pines and the stinging nettle have their pollen transported by the wind. The anthers produce masses of pollen which floats in the mildest breeze. Pollen from pine forests often forms a yellow coating on nearby lakes and ponds. Pine pollen grains have a small hollow compartment so that they can be carried on the wind like a kite.

When pollen lands on a sticky stigma, pollination takes place. The pollen grain grows a long tube down into the style until it reaches the ovary. Once there, the male cell travels down the tube and joins the egg. This is known as fertilisation. Gradually the ovary grows and the petals drop off the flower. They are not needed any more. Slowly the ovary grows into a fruit. The fruit is vital. The seeds inside it will grow into new plants.

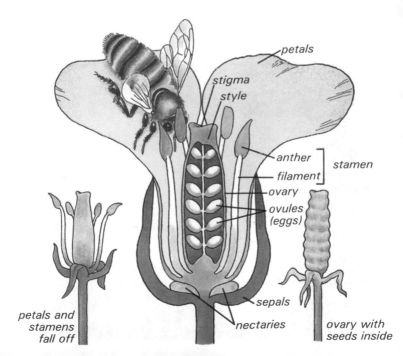

petals

stigma
style

anther
filament } stamen

ovary
ovules
(eggs)

sepals

nectaries

petals and
stamens
fall off

ovary with
seeds inside

Seeds

Some fruits, such as plums and cherries, have one large seed. Some plants, such as blackberry and strawberry, develop lots of seeds. The wild poppy has thousands of seeds, and dark mullein has over 700,000. A full grown mullein is about one metre across, and someone has calculated that if all its seeds germinated and grew to full size, the young of those plants would cover the whole of the British Isles. Think what would happen in the second year!

All seeds are covered with a seed coat. Look at a bean seed and you will see a scar and a tiny hole on the seed coat. The hole is where the seed will take in water, and the scar marks the point where it was joined to the parent plant. Split the bean open and inside you will find two seed leaves. These are the *cotyledons* which contain stored food. You will also see a shoot, called the *plumule*, and the root which is called the *radicle* (see page 24).

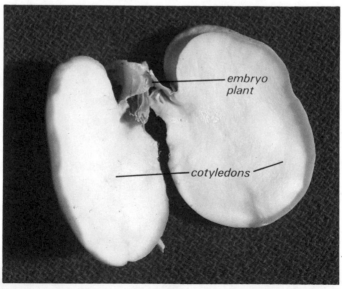

embryo plant

cotyledons

When the earth is warm and moist, seeds germinate: that is, begin to grow into new plants. Seeds do not grow immediately they land on the soil. Some are covered with hard shells, and do not grow until the tough casing rots. Apples and pears, with the seeds inside, lie on the ground until the soft flesh decays or is eaten by wild creatures. Other seeds, like cress, germinate quickly.

To grow cress, put a piece of dampened cotton wool or blotting paper on a saucer and sprinkle with cress seeds. Rest the saucer in a warm, dark place. The seeds will germinate and grow in a few days.

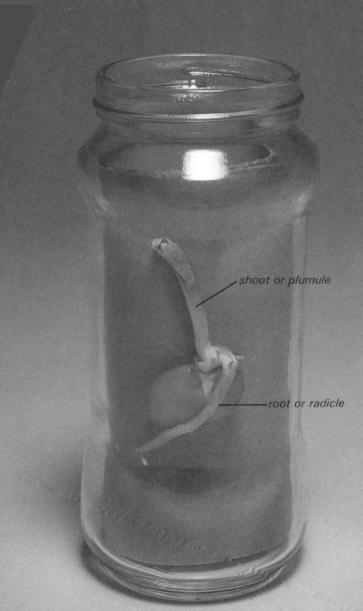

shoot or plumule

root or radicle

germinating bean seed showing development of shoot and root

Germination

It is very easy to grow most seeds at home if we provide moisture, warmth, and air, and put the seeds in a darkened area. What happens in a woodland, though, where the seeds cannot be carefully looked after? How does a pine tree, for example, survive and germinate?

The seeds of pine trees are tucked inside the woody cones, and, when the cone opens, the winged seeds gently float to the earth. Inside each seed is an *embryo*, which is the pine tree in its earliest form. Unlike an animal, which can move about freely in search of food and water, the pine seed is locked in place. It cannot move on its own. But it must have water and warmth before it begins to grow.

Over the winter the seeds get covered with dead leaves and needles from the woodland trees. With the coming of spring, the soil gets warmer, the rain softens the ground, and a change takes place in the seeds.

First the seed takes in water through the small hole in the seed coat. This makes the seed swell and splits the seed coat. Now more water can get in and the young root begins to grow. When the root goes into the soil, it can take up even more water. This helps the shoot to develop, and the young food leaves grow up towards the light in the sky, pushing off the unwanted seed case. The tree's life has begun.

Whichever way the pine seed lies on the forest floor, the shoot always makes its way upwards and the root downwards. You can watch this by growing beans in a jar. Line a jar with damp blotting paper and fill the middle with cotton wool. Push three beans between the blotting paper and the side of the jar, each set in a different position. Dampen the cotton wool and place the jar in a warm, dark cupboard. Look at it each day and see what is happening. The shoots grow upwards to push through the soil and reach the light, and the roots grow downwards.

Dispersal

Plants spread their seeds over the countryside. Fruits drop to the ground in the autumn and the fleshy skin rots away, leaving the seeds on top of the earth. Some berries are eaten by birds and the seeds land some distance away in the birds' droppings. Squirrels bury acorns as a winter food hoard, and those not eaten grow the following spring. Other seeds are blown by the wind and some float on streams and rivers.

Wind dispersal

Orchid and poppy seeds are small and light and they float in a current of air. Willow herb, groundsel and dandelions disperse their fruits and seeds on the air. The dandelion fruit has a parachute-shaped structure which carries the seeds far away from the parent plant. The sycamore and ash have wing-like seeds and when they fall from the trees they twirl in the air. If you come across a sycamore seedling in a woodland, find where the parent tree is growing. This will give you some idea of the distance a seed can move on the air.

Dispersal by explosion

Violets, and several plants in the pea family, spread their seeds by an explosion. The seeds develop in pods which dry in the summer. When the seeds are ripe, the pods twist and split open, scattering the seeds.

Animal dispersal

Some seeds and fruits cling to animals. Others are swallowed and pass through the creature unharmed. Ants collect some seeds for food and many of them germinate. When you walk through long grass, your clothes often pick up fruits that have hooks on them. Some seeds cling because they are sticky.

Water dispersal

This is not a common method of dispersing seeds. Water lily and marsh marigold seeds have air pockets which help them to float for some distance before they get water-logged and sink. Coconuts are encased in a waterproof coat and float, drifting on the sea for long distances.

New growth

The buttercup and wild strawberry develop *runners*, which are long, thin, spindly stems stretched over the woodland floor. Some distance away from the parent plant, a young strawberry plant develops on the runner and its weight presses the stem down to the earth. When the stem touches the soil, roots begin to grow and work their way into the topsoil. As this is taking place, the new plant continues to take food from the parent strawberry until it has a secure hold in the ground and starts making food in its own leaves. The runner then slowly dies and withers, leaving a new strawberry plant growing in the ground.

Have you ever seen thick clumps of bramble bushes? They develop in the wild because bramble bushes *tip root*. This means that when a tip of one branch touches the damp earth, it often makes new roots and so starts a new bramble plant. Bramble clumps provide homes for

tip root

countless small creatures, and nesting sites for robins and wrens.

New plants can grow from sections cut off the original plant. You can watch this happening if you dig up a dandelion plant with its tap root intact. Cut the root into several small pieces, and bury the sections separately in plant pots filled with damp soil. (See illustration (a) below.) Place the pots under a shaded greenhouse shelf or in a dark, warm cupboard. Check each week and see what happens. Don't let the pots dry out.

Gardeners take *cuttings* from healthy plants to increase their garden stock. You can try this with a geranium or fuchsia. Cut a tip about ten centimetres long from a strong vigorous plant, strip off the lower leaves, and plant the cutting in some soil mixed with sand. Keep the soil mixture moist and warm. Soon the cuttings will take root and grow into new plants. (See illustration (b) below.)

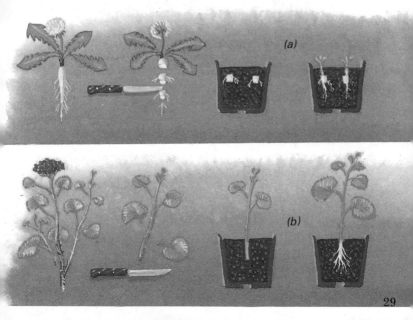

(a)

(b)

Annuals, biennials and perennials

Some plants live for one year. Others live for two or more. The red poppy grows and dies in one season, whilst an oak tree may live for centuries. Plants such as the poppy are *annuals*. An annual germinates, grows up, flowers, sets seeds and then dies. Such plants pass the winter safely as seeds.

Plants which live for two years are *biennials*. They grow from seed in the first season and develop food-making leaves. During the winter period, the biennial plant lies dormant in the ground until the spring. Then the plant grows again, feeding on food stored the previous year. Its flowers form the fruit and the seed, and the plant dies. The seeds are dispersed and, if they land on a suitable area, they germinate and the two-year cycle begins again.

Many flowering plants live for years. They are called *perennials*. Each year they grow and produce food during the spring and summer months. They rest during the winter.

Some perennials shed their leaves in the autumn, and some keep their leaves throughout the winter. Other perennials die back above the ground during the cold months, and keep a short, thick stem underground. This is called the *rootstock*.

Plants do not live for ever, although the bristlecone pine can live for over a thousand years.

a perennial root

Yarrow

Lupins

Primula

Scots Pine

Trees

Some trees shed their leaves in the autumn and lie
dormant in the winter months. They are called *deciduous*
trees. When spring arrives, deciduous trees grow new
replacement leaves.

Evergreen trees have leaves all year round. They grow
new ones on new twigs each spring, and the old leaves fall
off when they are worn out, whatever the time of year.

The fir and pine trees are evergreen, but not the larch.
They are called *conifers* which means they produce seeds
in cones. Conifers are usually fast growing and have tall,
straight trunks and needle-like leaves.

bark

annual rings

cambium

Trees are not a separate category of plants. A tree is a plant with a woody stem. Its stem (the trunk) is protected by the bark. As the tree grows, the trunk widens and the bark splits and cracks. Inside the bark there is the growing layer called the *cambium*. Each spring the cambium makes wood cells and bark cells, using water and mineral salts from the soil and carbon dioxide from the air. In summer the growth slows down and makes a darker ring of wood. These rings make a pattern of circles — one for each year of the tree's life. They are called *annual* rings. You can see them when a tree is cut down; if you count the rings it will tell you the age of the tree in years.

You can also tell something of the weather in past years from the rings. The good summers for tree growing will leave thicker rings than the summers which were poor.

Grass

Farmers say that grass is the very stuff of life. Grasses are a very important group of plants. We get cereals from grasses such as wheat, barley, oats, maize and rice. They are rich in starch and contain fats, proteins, minerals and vitamins that we need for a healthy life.

Thousands of years ago, man made a discovery that changed the course of history. He found that by growing certain kinds of wild grasses, he could harvest grain that could be ground into flour to make bread.

Grasses have flowers without petals. The leaves are called *blades* and are usually long and narrow. Some grasses are short and others tall. Bamboo is a grass which grows very high with stems as thick as tree trunks. Most grasses are perennial, although one very common type, annual meadow grass, grows in thick tufts which die back each year.

Grasses need water. To show the importance of water, an experiment was carried out in the USA on two plots of land, one of them irrigated and the other without irrigation. The dry land produced over fifty bushels of corn per hectare, while the other plot yielded twice as much.

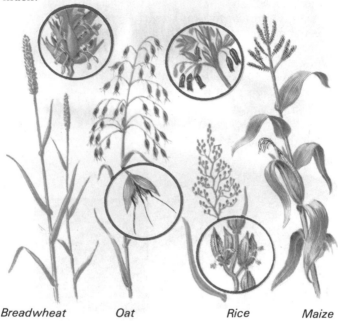

Breadwheat   Oat   Rice   Maize

One scientist made a study in which a single plant of winter rye grass was grown in a box that contained a cubic metre of soil. Over four months the plant grew fifty centimetres above the ground, but beneath the surface over three hundred and fifty kilometres of roots had formed to support the plant. Another man estimated that a corn plant uses five hundred litres of water during a hundred-day growth period!

What plants need

Plants, like all living things, need air, water, warmth and light. You can prove that plants need light by growing garden peas in small plastic pots, some in sunlight and some in dark, lightproof cupboards or boxes. All the peas will grow at first, and the peas in the dark will grow taller than those in the sunshine because they are searching for light. If the cupboard is lightproof, then the peas will die. The other peas carry on growing because their leaves trap the energy of the sunlight and use it to make food. Can you think of other experiments that prove plants need water and warmth to live?

One of the miracles of life is the way green plants use energy from the sun to make food. Green plants make food in their leaves by a process called *photosynthesis*.

plant makes sugars
to store as food

water and salts from soil

Plants need light, carbon dioxide from the air, and water and salts from the earth. Each leaf works like a tiny factory. Each one contains special cells which change the carbon dioxide and water into a form of sugar, using sunshine energy. At night, plants do not manufacture food. They keep alive by getting energy back from some of their own sugars, which were made during the daytime.

The green colour in the leaves is a substance called chlorophyll. It is this which captures the energy from sunlight which is needed to make the sugars. Photosynthesis also makes oxygen as well as sugars for the plant. This oxygen goes back into the air and replaces the oxygen which animals breathe in. Without it we would not be able to stay alive.

The green leaves manufacture food for the whole plant. Any surplus sugar is changed into starch which is stored, usually in the leaves. During the night the starch changes back to sugar and is carried by the veins away from the leaves. Extra food that is not used immediately by the growing and working parts of the plant is stored for future use in the stem or roots. Some is also kept in the leaves, the fruits and the seeds.

weathering breaks down rock

The soil

Soil is vital for plants. Good healthy soil produces strong, healthy plants. Its well-being is vital to the flowers, bushes and trees that depend on it. But where does the soil come from? Why doesn't it get worn out when so many plants grow in it, year after year?

Scientists have estimated that nature takes about five hundred years to create three centimetres of rich topsoil. The making of soil begins with rock. Rock is weathered by the action of water. Countless millions of raindrops slowly wear it away and dissolve the minerals it contains.

Lichens form on shattered rock

The snow, ice, wind and rain gradually break down rock into small particles which form the basis of new soil. Plants also help. Lichens secrete an acid that dissolves minerals in the rock. They form thin cracks into which moisture finds its way. In winter, the water freezes and expands, and some of the rock cracks off.

As the lichens die, their remains gather in the cracks and provide a rich layer in which mosses and ferns grow. *Humus*, (that is, dead leaves and rotting wood) broken down by minute creatures and underground fungi and bacteria, joins the mineral-rich particles to create a substance ideal for further plant growth.

Plants that do not flower

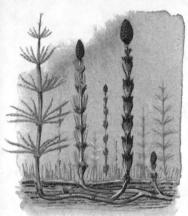

There are many plants growing in the wild that do not produce flowers. Mosses, horsetails, clubmosses, ferns and fungi are all non-flowering plants. Millions of years ago, when the Earth's climate was warmer and damper than it is today, these plants grew in larger numbers all over the world. As the climate slowly changed, many died away, leaving non-

Horsetail Fern

flowering plants that now live in moist, shady areas.

These plants do not produce flowers or seeds. Instead they grow from *spores* which develop in a *fruiting body*. Spores are small and light and float gently in a breeze. When they land on wet earth, they usually grow into new plants.

One of the smallest and most primitive plants is the *pleurococcus* which is an algae. Pleurococcus lives in clusters of single cells on damp wooden fences and tree trunks. Algae do not have roots, stems or leaves. As each cell grows, it splits into two parts, increasing the size of the colony. The cells stop growing during very dry spells of weather, and start again when the air is damp. Can you find algae in your garden?

Another simple algae is *spirogyra* which lives on the surface of ponds and canals. Spirogyra grows in tangled slimy clumps. If you separate out a single strand and look at it under a low-powered microscope, you will see a single strand or filament made up of

Pleurococcus

lots of cells joined together, end to end. Each cell has a fairly thick wall covered with a substance which makes the plant feel slimy. The spirogyra filament increases in length when its cells divide. Each new cell slowly grows in length to the normal size. If the plant is split, the parts carry on living as new and separate plants. Spirogyra does not need spores to reproduce.

Spirogyra

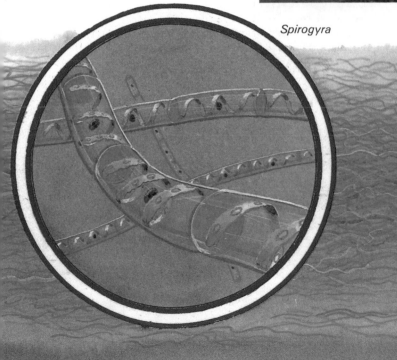

Mosses

Mosses thrive in damp woodlands, growing in clumps, often close to water. They are hardy plants and can live for a long time without water. Some live on mountains, on tree trunks, and in cracks between paving stones and bricks. They are among the first plants to live in barren places.

Mosses do not have flowers. Instead, they develop from tiny fertilised spores. When the spores are ripe (normally during springtime), the case splits and the spores are released into the air. New moss plants grow when the spores land on a suitable patch of ground. They have structures that resemble leaves, stem and roots. The roots are called *rhizoids*. These are hair-like structures that anchor the plant to the ground and absorb water and minerals. The stalk is called a *seta*. It supports the spore-producing capsule. Attached to the seta are leaf-like scales.

Sphagnum moss colonises bogs and swamps. Sphagnum has tiny holes in its leaves which suck up water. When the moss grows in a pool of water, its offspring grow on top of the dead mosses until the whole pond gets choked with sphagnum. As this becomes thicker and thicker, peat is eventually formed.

spore-producing capsule

seta

Perhaps the most common wall-living moss is the wall screw moss which is found in little tufts between old bricks and on undisturbed rocks. Growing next to wall screw moss, grey cushion moss can usually be seen. Rough-stalked feather moss lives on lawns that do not have a good drainage system.

Liverworts

Sometimes in damp areas of gardens you may find some flat and leather-like plants called *liverworts*. These are close relatives of mosses and the most common is the crescent cup liverwort, often found growing in greenhouses, especially in well-watered and undisturbed plant pots.

Liverwort

Ferns

Ferns are different from flowering plants. They do not produce flowers. In the autumn, fern leaves, known as *fronds*, develop small rows of powdery brown dots. These are spores which can grow into new plants.

You can grow ferns from spores if you provide the right conditions. Pick part of a ripe fern frond (that is, one with spores) and put it between two sheets of newspaper. Leave in a dry place. Meanwhile, prepare a compost from coarse sand and an equal quantity of peat. Quarter fill a clay pot with broken pot pieces (for drainage) and add the compost. Stand the pot in water until the peat is soaked. Gently scrape the dry spores onto the peat. Cover the pot with a plastic bag and place it in a shaded place.

Hart's-tongue Fern showing spores on underside

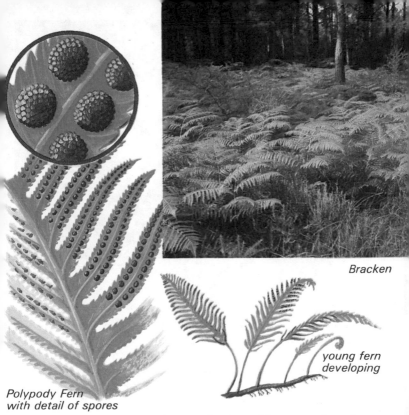

Bracken

young fern developing

Polypody Fern with detail of spores

Spores take a long time to develop. After several weeks each spore grows into a heart-shaped leaf called the *prothallus*. On the undersurface of the prothallus are minute roots and microscopic sex organs. Male cells fertilise the female parts. Then it may be up to a year before the first frond of the new fern appears. The fern plants must be thinned out as they grow in the pot.

Most ferns are tropical. Others live in shaded and damp places. Wall rue and maidenhair spleenwort grow on old, damp walls. The common polypody fern grows on garden walls and sometimes high up on tree trunks. The most common fern is bracken.

Field Mushroom

Fungi

Mushrooms, toadstools and moulds are *fungi*. They do not have true roots, leaves or chlorophyll and cannot make their own food. They live by feeding on other plants and animals. Fungi are nature's scavengers, slowly breaking down dead material and returning much of the goodness to the earth, helping to maintain the condition of the soil.

Toadstools are a common sight in the autumn. The part of each fungus that we see is the section that carries the spores. Underground there is a mass of hair-like structures called *hyphae* that act like roots, absorbing food and anchoring the fungus to the earth. When the time comes to make and release the wind-borne spores, the hyphae quickly grow above ground into a small round knob, on top of a stem, which soon changes into a curved cap typical of the ripe fungus.

If you place a fungus cap on a sheet of white paper, the spores drop onto the paper and leave a spore print.

Ink Cap

Check with a grown-up before picking or handling any fungi. Some are extremely poisonous. Always wash your hands after touching any fungi and dispose of the remains carefully after the experiment.

Sulphur Tuft

Lichens on tree bark

Lichens

Lichens live in rugged places. They grow on the roofs of old houses, on stone walls and on tree bark. Each lichen is a strange partnership of two different plants, an alga and a fungus. Look at a lichen under a microscope, and you will see a network of thin hair-like fungal strands that anchor the lichen to the ground. Tiny green algae give the colour to the plant.

Some lichen colonies look like a layer of fine powder stuck to rocks and large stones. These lichens are called *crustose* lichens. During hot, dry spells they stop growing but do not die. They can survive long periods in this state. *Foliose* lichens are leaf-shaped and usually grow on trees in damp woodlands, sometimes covering the bark completely. *Fruticose* lichens have small fruiting bodies that develop from the stalk.

Lichens are good indicators of air pollution. In industrial areas where there are unusual amounts of sulphur dioxide in the air, lichens die. In the worst areas, you will not find any lichens at all.

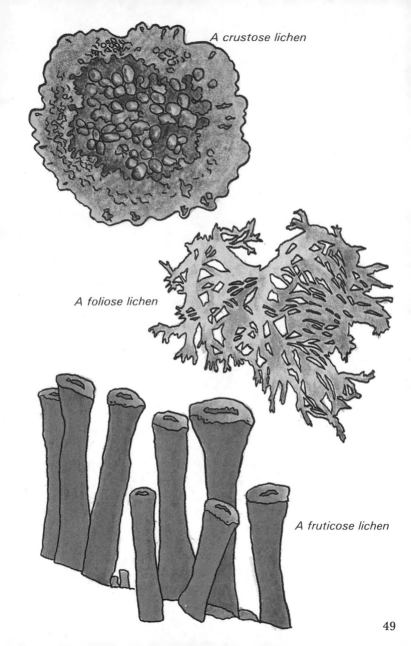

A crustose lichen

A foliose lichen

A fruticose lichen

49

Sundew

Unusual plants

Some plants trap and digest small creatures. The sundew, a plant living in marshy areas, has long, sticky growths that curl around insects. The sundew secretes digestive juices over its prey and feeds off it.

The leaves of the pitcher plant are curled to make a deep funnel with water at the bottom. The inside of the leaves is covered with a slippery wax and thousands of tiny hairs which point down towards the water. If an insect enters the plant it slides down into the water and cannot climb out. The insect drowns in the water, and the pitcher plant absorbs the juices of its prey.